BODl

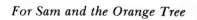

For Sam and the Orange Tree

James Saunders

BODIES

AMBER LANE PRESS

All rights whatsoever in this play are strictly reserved and
application for professional performance should be made
before rehearsal to:
Margaret Ramsay Ltd.,
14A Goodwin's Court,
St Martin's Lane,
London WC2N 4LL.

Application for amateur performance should be made to:
Samuel French Ltd.,
26 Southampton Street,
London WC2E 7JE.

No performance may be given unless a licence has been
obtained.

First published in 1979 by
Amber Lane Productions Ltd.,
Amber Lane Farmhouse,
The Slack,
Ashover, Derbyshire S45 0EB.

Printed in Great Britain by
A. Wheaton & Co. Ltd., Exeter.

Typesetting and make-up by
Computerset (Phototypesetting) Ltd., Oxford.

Bodies was originally commissioned by the Richmond Fringe Theatre at Richmond's Orange Tree, London and received its world premiere there on 29 April, 1977. It was directed by Sam Walters, with the following cast:

ANNE	Ruth Goring
DAVID	Geoffrey Beevers
HELEN	Isobil Nisbet
MERVYN	Rio Fanning

A revised version of *Bodies* was presented at the Hampstead Theatre, London on 20 February, 1978. It was directed by Robin Lefèvre and designed by Tanya McCallin, with the following cast:

ANNE	Gwen Watford
DAVID	David Burke
HELEN	Anne Stallybrass
MERVYN	Dinsdale Landen

The Hampstead Theatre production was transferred to the Ambassadors Theatre, London on 23 April, 1979, with the following cast:

ANNE	Gwen Watford
DAVID	David Burke
HELEN	Angela Down
MERVYN	Dinsdale Landen

Characters in order of appearance

ANNE

HELEN

DAVID

MERVYN

In Act One the action takes place in the respective living rooms of Anne and Mervyn and of Helen and David. Act Two is set in the living room of Anne and Mervyn the following Saturday.

ACT ONE

[ANNE *enters.*]

ANNE: I was never, thank God, an Idealist; no romantic; the dewy-eyed approach irritated me. I suppose the parents contributed, with their talk of love and niceness, their comfy-cosiness, covering a shoddy making-do with each other. My first period, I thought: so that's what's behind it all — *this* discomfort, *this* mess. And these things sprouting in front, these impositions, to be hiked about, hawked about through life in case I should happen to breed. The nerve! Pretty brash cynicism; but better that way than the other. Useful too, a good defence, it gave me an edge, I used it when the time came, when the occasion warranted. 'I'm having a period, do you mind!' They minded, mostly; well, at that age. Another trick I had, toffees in the handbag; faced with an importunate male at the end of a dreary evening he thought I should pay for, I'd pop a Sharp's Kreemy into my mouth and start chewing. That spiked the romantic gun, at the expense of a filling or two. Or both together, the ultimate deterrent.
      [*She talks as if chewing toffee.*]
      'I'm having a period, do you mind!' I grew out of it, of course, matured; I mean I learned to enjoy myself, take what was available, including *romance,* why not? Feet on the ground, though, head below the clouds. I thought I was unfoolable, set for life. My expectations were never more than reasonable, before and after marriage, I anticipated difficulties, and got

9

them; I coped. His first infidelity — though I didn't believe in the concept — I pushed out of sight, refusing to be disturbed. And the others. And then, well into what I thought was my maturity, coming up forty would you believe, the cataclysm. The mess. The mess of it. I was not unhappy, that was the point, not dissatisfied as far as I knew, there were no great blisses but what do you expect, *I* expected nothing more; and then, out of nowhere, the first intimations: a restlessness, a strange unease, like the feeling you have before you know you're going to be sick. I increased my activity, became rather manic, threw a big party; I hated to be alone, doing nothing; time was going by so quickly, suddenly, *had* gone by, forty years of it, probably more than I had left. My time was running out, I had to use it, mark it with my brand. Something in me started looking for a meaning, a value that would give meaning, to make it all right that I was getting older and would die, die and lose everything. Be lost. Then it focussed, oh so suddenly, or I became aware of it suddenly, focussed on someone I'd known for years, one of our closest friends, David of David and Helen, our old buddies who lived in our pockets and we in theirs. It was ridiculous; ludicrous . . .

[HELEN *enters.*]

HELEN: I'd felt for some time there was something odd, something out of key, a vague disquiet; I thought it was me. Because on the face of it things were going better than usual with us. We were doing more together, going out a lot, entertaining, seeing a lot of Mervyn and Anne. We'd always gone very well together, the four of us. David and Mervyn were old buddies, and the first time I ever met Anne I knew we'd be good friends. I looked up to her, she was older than me. I looked up to her. We saw each other constantly about that time, the two of us or the four of us: coffee, shopping, PTA, cinema, drinks, meals, parties, a lot of parties around then. One evening Anne rang. She wanted to see a film, Mervyn wanted to stay in, would I like to come. I said I couldn't, I had something to do; I suggested David. 'Oh, yes,' she said, 'If he'd *like* to.' I put him on the phone, thinking perhaps I'd said the wrong thing: she sounded rather uncertain. Then David: 'Yes, all right. Yes, that will be quite nice.' Casual, rather offhand. He put the phone down. He had a large scotch before he went. Halfway through the evening the penny suddenly dropped. I realised I'd known for some time. He came back saying how dull the film had been; they'd had a coffee afterwards. It had been going on for months.

[DAVID *enters.*]

DAVID: It seemed rather a small thing at the time. Don't misunderstand; there was an intensity there, a great physical attraction; but it didn't seem — important, not vital, just something I felt would be nice to happen, something I fancied. Things were going smoothly enough marriage-wise. The job was — all right, not unpleasant, not uninteresting on the whole, I was doing quite well, on my way up; and domestic-wise — well, as I say. Kids set problems, of course, of course they do, it's part of the game; but no great hassles, no great dramas; we coped reasonably well together, we all did. And I had my extra interest, if things got too much, the creative outlet, the painting. There were occasional frustrations there, I suppose: trying to go beyond my talent, the odd loss of confidence, but that's part of the process. Again, I don't want to exaggerate, I didn't suffer with it. I was no Van Gogh, thank God, and knew it. A Sunday

11

painter, I suppose; nothing wrong with that; if someone called it a hobby I didn't object. What I'm getting
at is this: if at the time, when the thought first came
into my head, when I first became aware of the attraction, the possibility — if then I'd thought through the
possible consequences, the complications, I'd have
said forget it then, sod it, I can do without it, I'll stay as
I am, thank you very much.

[MERVYN *enters.*]

MERVYN: I don't know when it started. I'd always assumed she
was an attractive woman — most women are; but I'd
never *noticed* she was. I began to remember details
about her, the way a painter would, the shape of the
fingernails, the colour of the eyes, the way she held her
head, and the details had a kind of value, as they
would to a painter. I'm not observant, I've always
dreaded witnessing a crime, seeing the robbers leave
the bank, being asked by the police: 'What exactly
happened, what time was it, what did the man look
like, was he wearing a hat, was he clean-shaven, is this
him?' So it was unusual, how she came into focus; I
could have painted her from memory — if I could
paint. Then I found I enjoyed talking to her, just me
with just her, without the usual worry: 'Am I boring
you, do you really want to be talking to me?' She
listened, listened very intently, watching my mouth,
letting me talk, hanging on my lips you might say, it
was very pleasing. I found I was flirting with her; she
was an old friend, the others were always there, it was
an unspoken joke between us, no harm in it . . . One
night we were coming back from the theatre, the four
of us, in my car. Anne was in the back with David,
Helen in front with me. I could hear them talking
behind me, about the play, about theatre. Helen was
quiet. I had a feeling I'd had before, of something

passing between us; something was being said. She lit me a cigarette, put it in my mouth, her fingers touched my lip for a moment. The silence went on, while the others chattered in the back. I flashed a look at her face; she was watching my hand on the wheel, very intently. That's when I realised that she — desired me, and I her, and that we both knew; that the way was open. The tension was extraordinary. I changed gear, and left my hand there as if casually, the back of the hand brushing her skirt.

[DAVID *is reading.*]

HELEN: Guess who rang today.

DAVID: Hm?

HELEN: Guess who rang up today ... Mervyn.

DAVID: Mervyn and Anne, Mervyn?

HELEN: Yes.

DAVID: Well, well ... What on earth made him do that after all this time?

HELEN: He said he'd heard we were back in England, and thought he'd give us a ring.

DAVID: I'm surprised.

HELEN: I was.

DAVID: How are they both? Well?

HELEN: I think so.

DAVID: Still living in the same place?

HELEN: Mm.

DAVID: Old Mervyn ... It would be nice to see them again.

HELEN: Do you think so?

DAVID: Why don't we?

HELEN: It's a long time.

DAVID: What is it — eight years?

HELEN: Nine.

DAVID: Do you think they'd like to see us? We could ask them over.

HELEN: Actually they've asked us. For a meal on Saturday. I said a provisional yes.

DAVID: Fine. We're not doing anything Saturday, are we?

HELEN: No.

DAVID: Funny, I was thinking about them only the other day.

HELEN: Were you?

DAVID: Something reminded me. It'll be interesting, seeing them again.

HELEN: Talking over old times?

DAVID: Hardly, I should think. Are you not sure about it?

HELEN: What do *you* think?

DAVID: It suits me.

HELEN: What are you reading?

DAVID: Detective.

HELEN: Good?

DAVID: Hm.

HELEN: Do you want to go out tonight?

DAVID: Where to?

HELEN: Cinema?

DAVID: I'm quite content to stay in. Are you going?
[*Slight pause.*]

HELEN: I might.

DAVID: Is he still at the same school?

HELEN: We didn't talk much. He had to ring off, some crisis. I think he said he's a headmaster now.

DAVID: I think I'll ring him up.

HELEN: No, don't do that.

DAVID: Why not?

HELEN: I said I'd ring back. He said no, I'll call you tomorrow. He was ringing from school. So I'm to say yes.

DAVID: Yes, why not?

HELEN: There are all sorts of possible reasons why not.

DAVID: Not now, surely. I'm quite looking forward to it; seeing old Mervyn again.

HELEN: And old Anne again.

DAVID: Yes.

HELEN: Whoever *they* are.

DAVID: I don't suppose they'll have changed much. Nine years isn't all that long.

HELEN: That's just it. They won't have, we will have. They'll be the first of the old friends we'll have met since coming back. Rather going in at the deep end.

DAVID: It's always interesting, renewing old ties.

[HELEN *gives a little cough.*]

You know what I mean. No danger of *that*.

HELEN: [*fey*] You know you may do as you like, darling. [*She smiles.*] It's odd, isn't it, that now we may both do as we like, we no longer want to?

DAVID: We do do as we like.

HELEN: *You* know what *I* mean.

[*She kisses his forehead lightly.*]

ANNE: It was bad. It got worse. I felt as if I were being taken over. Part of me of course wanted to be, wanted to give over control. And the arguments with myself: I'd be taking nothing from Mervyn; on the contrary, I'd be replenishing myself, it would be good for our relationship, make me a better wife. Perhaps I'd learn a new trick or two. Forgetting he'd said rather similar things to me, from time to time. At least I'd keep it to myself, at least I wouldn't come crawling home to confess, shove it on his shoulders, as he used to: 'Darling, I have something to tell you . . .' Or moon about with that hangdog look of guilt on him, forcing me to prise it out of him, not having the courage, or the decency, to take his own responsibility, to take the trouble even to lie properly. Always imagining, it seemed — I never understood the stupidity of this — always imagining the time would come when I'd say: 'You poor darling, how difficult it must be for you, I see how you need it, you must have it of course, you must be yourself, I quite understand.' At least, I told myself I'd never do that; if David went with deception, that was the price to pay. And if he did find out, if there was even the danger, I'd stop. I was quite definite on that. And anyway — I said — I know there's a revenge in it, a getting my own back for various things; but better out than in. Better this little revenge that does him no harm than a soured, bitter life later on. I'd be doing him a favour; and myself. Too many reasons. We all had too many reasons. I shuffled the cards, laying them out like a fortune-teller, trying to find the arrangement which would say: don't blame yourself; stop struggling; there's nothing you can do; it's ordained. Well, ordained or not, I went ahead and did it.

DAVID: That wasn't straight. To say it didn't seem important, to say it was just something I fancied, to say if I'd seen the difficulties I'd have done without — that was how I thought *then*, how I kidded myself. The part I played then, the act I put on, was of the carelessly trendy rising young executive; but — this was the clever part — not obsessed by it, not taken over, always my own man. I wasn't *in* the rat race, I just used the machinery to earn a living. Agreed, I'd say, arguing with Mervyn, the business ethic is a questionable thing, or at least a frivolous thing; of course I know marketing paper products is a strange use of energy; but so's cricket a strange use of energy. It's only a game — for me; I don't take it seriously, as you do teaching; and you don't believe in the education system. So with the painting: I'd never allow I was serious at it. I was everyone's man, and no-one's. I was, of course, terrified: of not being noticed, not being praised, not being liked, loved, admired, of being caught backing a losing cause. Of not existing; and no-one ever

16

guessed, least of all me. I was certainly no Van Gogh;
but I suffered, suffered the pain of not being told at
every moment that I was *necessary*. To business, to art,
to Mervyn, to Helen — and then to Anne. As soon as I
saw that to her I was an object of desire, I was done for;
I had to be the best, the greatest, the only, the necessary
lover.

MERVYN: Crisis today.

ANNE: Oh? What happened?

MERVYN: We had the police round.

ANNE: Not again. Shoplifting?

MERVYN: No, worse. You remember Simpson?

ANNE: Your weird sixth-former? Drugs?

MERVYN: No. He tried to kill himself.

ANNE: Oh my God.

MERVYN: Well, it seems that way. There were two witnesses. He
drove his motor-bike straight into a wall. Revved up,
and went straight into it.

ANNE: It could have been an accident. Perhaps he skidded.

MERVYN: He didn't skid. He had perfect control. They both said
it looked totally deliberate. It was a straight road. He's
had the bloody bike two years, he knows how to use it.
And he'd left his helmet off.

ANNE: How is he?

MERVYN: He's in a coma. They've got him on one of those life-
support systems. He's not expected to come off it.
[*He breaks a little.*]

ANNE: Were you fond of him?

MERVYN: I hated the sod ... No I didn't; I was sorry for him.

ANNE: Do you know why he did it?

MERVYN: The reason I'm a bit ... The reason the police called
round — with his father — was that it happened
yesterday straight after school. During school in fact.
He had a blank last period. Instead of going to the
common room as he usually did, he went straight out

and did it. So he wasn't drunk, and he wasn't drugged.

ANNE: Did you see him yesterday?

MERVYN: Yes. The last thing he was at was the English seminar.

ANNE: Your seminar.

MERVYN: Yes.

ANNE: Did anything happen?

MERVYN: No.

ANNE: How did he seem?

MERVYN: As usual. He asked his usual damn-fool questions.

ANNE: What about?

MERVYN: Oh, what does it matter? He never got any answers. I don't think he expected any. I don't think there are any. I think that's why he asked them. Awkward bugger. With your normal student, if he's doing English literature he does English literature, if he's doing philosophy he does philosophy — he doesn't want bloody connections all the time, bloody relevances . . . I remember once when *I* was at school, one of the other kids said to the maths teacher, 'Sir, I don't see the point in algebra; what's it for?' The teacher said: 'What it's for is for doing in my class; and why you do it is because I tell you. Now do it.' I thought that was a good answer.

ANNE: Did you?

MERVYN: Well . . . it simplifies things . . . He was obsessed with the minor Victorian poets, can you believe it?

ANNE: Simpson?

MERVYN: Perhaps he identified. He wrote poetry.

ANNE: Any good?

MERVYN: I don't think so. Those young late-Victorian lay-abouts, the *Tragic Generation* somebody called them: Lord Alfred Douglas and Dowson and Symons and the rest; commuting between London and Paris on a pittance; a slim volume of mediocre verse, wispy stuff, what one of my lecturers used to call 'romanticism

strained through a silk stocking'; much discussion of
Art and a few fucked chorus girls, that was their life.

ANNE: You get very reactionary when you're upset.

MERVYN: I wouldn't think you'd have much sympathy with
that lot, do you?

ANNE: They don't bother me.

MERVYN: His sixty-four dollar question this time was: 'Which is
more valuable, a poet's life or his poetry?' I said,
'Valuable to whom?' He said, 'Do you mean value is
subjective?' I said, 'Of course it is, or there'd be no-one
to evaluate it.' He said, 'I was reading some Ernest
Dowson. He had a wretched life, he died at thirty-two,
and he left one or two good poems.' He said, 'Do you
think it would have been better if he'd lived a contented life and not written any poetry?' I said, '*I* think
not, obviously, because he's dead and his poetry is still
around.' Then he said, 'So you do value poetry higher
than life.' I said, 'I don't think I said that. Now do you
think we could get back to literature and leave the
metaphysics for some other time?' He said, 'Yes, all
right.' And walked out.

ANNE: Oh ... What was it, a cry for help?

MERVYN: Oh, don't be fatuous.

ANNE: Or a suicide note.

MERVYN: Maybe it *was* an accident. That's what his father
wants to believe.

ANNE: Did you tell the father about the seminar?

MERVYN: No, of course not. It probably had nothing to do with
it. He was always trying to be profound. Bloody
pseud. If it was a cry for help he was asking rather a
lot. Anyway, he's stopped asking now.

[ANNE *looks sharply at him.*]

I've still got a book he lent me. He kept asking if I'd
read it. I don't know whether to give it back.

ANNE: I wouldn't.

MERVYN: Darling, I've got something else to tell you.

        [ANNE *freezes.*]

        David and Helen are back in England. I've invited them to a meal on Saturday. Is that all right?

HELEN: The first thing I felt was anger at myself. It was so obvious. I thought back. It was so obvious. What a fool I was. What a fool they must take me for. And how many others knew? Mervyn, surely, or is he as big a fool as me? Then at them, the anger: my husband, to take my best friend; my best friend, to take my husband. How could they? To betray me, so thoughtlessly, so blatantly. It was vile. And for what? To fuck one another. To fuck one another they'd betray me, betray Mervyn, betray the friendship. What was it, to make them do that? What did they have, what did they get to pay for it? What was it they had together to do that for? Then the self-pity: I was betrayed, I was rejected, I had no-one, I was nothing, there was no-one I could trust, there was no trust, there was no value. There was nothing but getting what you wanted; nothing else. Then the revenge. I'll have *him*. I'll have him, I'll have hers.

MERVYN: Back of the hand barely touching the skirt. God, I thought, they must feel it back there, the waves of it, like bloody D-Day! After that it was torment. Of course it was totally impossible: her best friend, the wife of my best friend; we lived practically in each other's pockets. It was mad. I tried to rationalise it away. I said: it's obvious what's happened. She's rather fallen for me for some reason, after all this time, perhaps they're having trouble; she's dissatisfied, looking around for something else. But that's her business. I don't have to follow suit. I'm flattered, that's all it is, because she wants me at a time when I don't feel particularly wanted. Don't be a fool, don't

behave like a child. Keep clear. Forget it. It'll go away.
I knew the cost of it, I was no beginner: the sick excite-
ment, the lurchings, the constant planning, the
tearing in two; a few islands of extraordinary happiness in a waste of messy discomfort. I've wondered
since whether I could have stood out against it. I don't
know, I suppose I could, I was a rational human
being, part of me anyway. The letting go is always a
conscious decision, whatever they say. What tipped
the balance, as before, as always, was first, an anger.
How dare things be this way! That the simple, good
coming together of two people is made an act of mad-
ness! Then a fear. I was afraid of losing something of
myself, afraid, in a way, of dying. The need, the desire,
whatever it was, was *my* experience; it was real, however painful it was, however perverse, it was mine, it
was me, it was the only real thing about me, that awful
obsessive clawing, the clawing of that need to be
myself, to do what needed to be done if I were not to
kill part of myself by killing that need. So I did it; or it
was done. One day I let go.

DAVID: By the way, Mervyn rang while you were out.

HELEN: Oh, did he?

DAVID: I said we'd be there. Eight o'clock.

HELEN: Good . . .

DAVID: He didn't recognise my voice; he thought he'd got the
wrong number.

HELEN: Your voice has softened.

DAVID: Have you noticed that?

HELEN: Oh yes . . . Did he say anything?

DAVID: They're both quite well. He *is* a head teacher now. So
of course he's not doing much teaching.

HELEN: That seems a pity. I imagine he was a good teacher.

DAVID: He'd have used a lot of energy. It's not necessarily the
same thing.

HELEN: I know it's not. I said I imagine he was a good teacher.

DAVID: Yes, I expect he was . . . Then he asked how we were . . .

HELEN: Did you tell him?

DAVID: What?

HELEN: How we are.

DAVID: You mean about the therapy?

HELEN: Yes.

DAVID: Yes, I told him about that. You don't mind, do you?

HELEN: No, of course not.

DAVID: I didn't go into details.

HELEN: It doesn't matter. They'll see we've changed. You like people to know, don't you?

DAVID: I don't see any point in keeping it secret.

HELEN: I mean you like to talk about it. You like to tell people how well you are.

DAVID: I don't boast about it.

HELEN: No.

DAVID: Odd coincidence. When I mentioned the therapy he said he'd been lent the book.

HELEN: Has he read it?

DAVID: I think so.

HELEN: We'll have something to live up to.

DAVID: You're not worried about seeing them, are you?

HELEN: It'll be strange. They'll be the same people they were. They'll expect us to be. It'll be like meeting our old selves again. I wonder why they want to see us.

DAVID: Friendship . . .

HELEN: I'm not so sure of myself as you are. I don't want to hurt them and I don't want to be hurt. It'll upset me if they're in a mess. It'll still upset me. I'm not that cured. You want to show them how well you've come out of it, don't you? How sane you are; how balanced.

DAVID: I don't think so.

HELEN: Why do you want to go then? They've got nothing to

give us. They'll just remind us.

DAVID: We should be able to face that. I think you're making too much of it. It'll be a pleasant evening.

HELEN: I suppose you're right. A touch of the old sinking feeling; something unresolved somewhere. We'll either enjoy it or not enjoy it. There's nothing else, is there?

ANNE: The beauty of it; my God, the beauty of it; when we first made it. All that need, all the accumulated energy of that need for him, which had been like a sickness, suddenly to be used, used, used . . . Only, afterwards, a day or two later, the need was there again. And now there were two things: the need again, and the memory of what it was like to lose it. And still I'd die, still my time was passing, it didn't stop that, just increased the urgency of it. I'd count the times, count the weeks that passed, live weeks or dead weeks: a live week, with him in it, a dead week without. I watched over my time like an accountant, the losses and gains, the wastage, the profit. The balance was always out, they all became dead weeks — they were all lost when I'd had them, good or bad; they left nothing, nothing but the need and the desire, nothing but more evidence of the only time I had passing, time dying, leaving need, more need. I grew voracious. I hunted my time like a wild animal, tore at it, wolfed it down. One evening, I came back from David, Mervyn was in bed, reading; I fell on him, tore love from him.

HELEN: Rather like an old film I've seen before. I still run it now and then, like an old home movie, run it through my mind, for amusement or — some reason; not from necessity, the obsession is gone. I watch the antics of the participants, their funny goings on, watch their mouths turn up and down, open and close . . . A nearly silent film, most of the words are gone, a few shreds come back ... [*She looks upward.*] ... not possible, we shall have to ... out of the house you cow ... oh God do that oh God do that oh God do that oh God ... [*She laughs.*] Rushes from an abandoned B-movie. And through it all the mouths open and close; all those words, so serious, so heartfelt, all those lies, all that desperate honesty, trying to explain, trying to understand, trying to justify; all gone, wiped off. Together with whatever powered it, the engine of it. Just a recollection left of pain and delight; it seemed to be all pain and delight; and the two, from here, oddly similar ...

MERVYN: Simpson's father rang again today. I met him for a drink on the way home.

ANNE: I wondered why you were late.

MERVYN: I tried to ring. You were engaged.

ANNE: What did he want?

MERVYN: To talk. So I let him.

ANNE: Did it help?

MERVYN: I don't know.

ANNE: What does he do?

MERVYN: Some sort of business man. He has to make a decision about his son.

ANNE: What?

MERVYN: They want to switch off the machine. I asked him to let me know.

ANNE: Why?

MERVYN: I don't know ... I rang David today, by the way.

ANNE: Oh?

MERVYN: They *are* coming on Saturday. I said eight o'clock.

ANNE: Right.

MERVYN: That's all right, is it?

ANNE: You've done it now, haven't you?

MERVYN: You think it's a mistake? You only have to say so. Sometimes you make me feel like a schoolboy waiting outside the headmaster's study.

ANNE: You *are* the headmaster. You're in charge.

MERVYN: It doesn't feel like it to me . . . I was always terrified of authority figures, and now I am one it doesn't make any difference. I tell you, I spend most of my energy at school hiding that dark secret from everyone, kids and staff — that under this forbidding exterior there's a quivering schoolboy, waiting eternally outside the head's study. That's why I come home so tired . . . I'm not in charge, I don't know who the hell is, but it's not me. At least at home I don't have to pretend it is.

ANNE: It's certainly not me.

MERVYN: Maybe no-one is. We're up shit creek in a barbed wire canoe without a captain.

ANNE: So you're disclaiming responsibility.

MERVYN: For what?

ANNE: Whatever you think I'm upset about. Whatever you feel guilty about.

MERVYN: Is that what I'm doing?

ANNE: As usual. You've always done that; said you were not responsible — in some vague way I can't argue against.

MERVYN: So I'm unoriginal. Don't throw my guilt at me. That *is* the dirty trick. I have guilt whether I'm guilty or not. I'm built on guilt. Guilt-built. You know that.

ANNE: You did it over her.

MERVYN: What?

ANNE: Is that what it is? You're so guilt-stricken you have to find things to use it up on? You did the same thing over her. 'You can't blame me, I'm not responsible for my actions.'

MERVYN: I never said that.

ANNE: The destruction caused in this world by people who act in spite of themselves.

MERVYN: You're not blameless, are you?

ANNE: Where I'm not blameless I take the blame. That's the difference.

MERVYN: I never said I wasn't responsible.

ANNE: Not so simply.

MERVYN: There's a difference between taking responsibility for one's actions and being able to change them.

ANNE: What?

MERVYN: I mean I was *impelled* ...

ANNE: You couldn't help yourself.

MERVYN: Not that, not that! I mean ... What I mean is, I wish you'd listen to me. What I mean is, being the kind of man I am, I can't find it in myself to — cancel out that impulse, to kill it, even if I could, I don't know whether I could, but even if I could ... But I still, though I can't help the kind of man I am, was, feel I must take — responsibility for what I do. You see it's not that simple.

ANNE: And do it all the same.

MERVYN: If I can stand it, yes, I'm afraid, if I can stand the consequences, yes.

ANNE: Good for you.

MERVYN: Which, I may say for your reassurance, takes more stamina than I have any more, more — more something.

ANNE: Libido?

MERVYN: Don't give me that psychoanalytical shit.

ANNE: You prefer to wrap it up in your own *special* jargon don't you, so it seems to have some sort of value. As if you're doing mankind a favour, leading it to greater heights. Instead of just saying: 'I wanted to have it off, so I had it off.'

MERVYN: Is that how you thought of you and David?

ANNE: How else?

MERVYN: I don't believe you.

ANNE: Please yourself.

[*Pause.*]

MERVYN: I wish to God I hadn't invited them now.

ANNE: It's a bit late to say that. So it's just your lack of stamina that's stopping you now? Are you getting past it at last?

MERVYN: I didn't say it was just my lack of stamina.

ANNE: Sorry, I thought you did. If you were a little less convoluted perhaps we'd understand each other better.

MERVYN: Life isn't simple.

ANNE: You can say that again. Why *did* you invite them?

MERVYN: I heard they were back in England so I rang them, that's all.

ANNE: Without letting me know.

MERVYN: I did let you know.

ANNE: After you'd arranged it.

MERVYN: I could have put them off today if you'd told me you didn't want to see them.

ANNE: What? 'I'm sorry, but Anne doesn't want to see you?'

MERVYN: It was an impulse. I rang them on the spur of the moment. I do that little enough nowadays, God knows.

ANNE: Did you have their number?

MERVYN: I knew they were living in Esher. So I rang directory enquiries.

ANNE: From school. All on an impulse.

MERVYN: Anyway, if I'd mentioned it first you'd have put it off. You'd have said, 'Oh, later, later.' We'd never have seen them.

ANNE: Now we're getting to it. You are a devious bugger. You've got some purpose in mind; you're up to something, aren't you?

MERVYN: All I've done is invite a couple of friends round for the evening.

ANNE: They're not friends. One thing necessary for friendship is communication, and we haven't communicated for years.

MERVYN: We send Christmas cards to each other. We never actually fell out with them.

ANNE: Don't be naive . . . And you're so bad at being devious. It always shows. It always did. That forced casualness, the hooded look in the eyes. You don't know how transparent you are.

MERVYN: That's *my* misfortune.

ANNE: Mine.

MERVYN: Whereas you can deceive me and I know nothing about it.

ANNE: Deceive you? Where? When? What are you talking about? I haven't deceived you for years.

MERVYN: Nor I you.

ANNE: I know you haven't. I don't need telling. When I deceive I do it properly.

MERVYN: When you tell me you do it properly too, don't you?

ANNE: Oh God, we're not going over all this again, are we? Why do you have to rake it all up?

MERVYN: I'm not raking it up. It's there already, it's there all the time, you know that. You want to write it all off, don't you, pretend it didn't really happen, have nothing more to do with it. I can't do that if you can.

ANNE: I'm not asking you to. Just keep it to yourself.

MERVYN: You want us to behave as if we'd never met them.

ANNE: I wish to God we hadn't.

MERVYN: Everything would have been all right then, wouldn't it? Everything would have gone swimmingly, if we'd just not met them.

ANNE: Oh, I don't know . . . I just don't want to think about it. Sometimes I feel like a clockwork toy that's been wound up and set in a particular direction and off I've gone on my clockwork legs. When I think of the time and energy I've spent trying to change things, trying to sort things out, it just makes me angry. Wasted effort. I might just as well let things happen, they do anyway. I don't want to be reminded of all that wasted effort. I don't know why you want reminding of it.

MERVYN: I don't like unfinished things.

ANNE: You think it's not finished?

MERVYN: Nothing ever finished. There was an explosion; nothing finished, nothing was resolved.

ANNE: So what do you expect to happen on Saturday?

MERVYN: I don't know.

ANNE: Right.

MERVYN: Strange thing. You know this book Simpson lent me?

ANNE: No.

MERVYN: I told you. It's about a new type of psychotherapy that's going in the States. And David and Helen have had it.

ANNE: Both of them?

MERVYN: Mm.

ANNE: Why did he tell you that?

MERVYN: He happened to mention it.

ANNE: People don't normally tell all and sundry they've been in analysis, do they?

MERVYN: It's not analysis. It's quite different. I've read the book.

ANNE: I just wondered if they're blaming us for it.

MERVYN: He didn't *put* it like that. Apparently he had a complete breakdown.

ANNE: When?

MERVYN: A few years ago.

ANNE: Has it done them any good, this therapy?

MERVYN: He says it has.

ANNE: Bully for them.

MERVYN: He talked about being cured.

ANNE: What of? Us?

MERVYN: We were probably just a symptom.

ANNE: Delightful.

DAVID: It became impossible. After the break-up, the change of partners, the break-up again, the reunion — all terribly serious, as if it were something of significance — after that we got the hell out. I had a chance in the States, we honestly thought we could start again. Dishonestly thought. 'Let's make a fresh start, leave the past behind us.' That's how we might have put it, following the old pattern. It couldn't work, of course, we carried our old selves with us, on our backs. Carried each other. We pussy-footed around for a time, being terribly gentle with each other, very courteous and polite and considerate; as if we were leading each other across water covered with very thin ice. Yes, that's the way it was: we crept about gingerly, pretending not to notice that under our feet the ice creaked. And then, for me, gave way. And I was in. That was the end of the pretence that we lived in a solid world. It was like going into icy water: first the awful humiliating shock of giving way, going in headlong, thrashing about; then the acceptance, that I was engulfed in this new medium, no question of escape, no toeholds, no fingerholds; I gave myself up, with relief, to drowning. But they pulled me out, laid me in white in an antiseptic environment, some place or other. The firm paid, with bad grace I think; but they honoured their obligations — written in; brought me to dry land, put me carefully back in the swim — [*He gives a little laugh.*] — in the shallows, where I'd do no harm. I knew they'd never promote me, of course, not after going through the ice. My limits were set; I might survive, with care. We lived timidly again, looking after each other, aware of the water swirling about underneath, the ice creaking. Then I read about the method; the therapy. It was supposed to work; well, we had nothing to lose.

MERVYN: Came the time when I realised Anne knew; and a new ritual set in. Having to make excuses for absence, knowing they weren't believed. 'Stopped for a drink on the way, met so-and-so' — knowing she knew I lied. But the game had to be played out. 'Oh, how is he? What did he say?' 'Fine, I think. Nothing of interest. Sends his regards.' She knew; I knew she knew; she knew I knew she knew. We played the game, terrified of what would happen if it came into the open. And taking it with me when I went to see her — Helen. Taking, I mean, Anne's — suffering. I tried not to call it that, but there was no other word for it. Suffering. Her suffering which I caused. Did I stop? No; I went on: more, it drove me from the house, I tried to escape from it, if it was only for an hour or two. Made love to *her;* and it was beautiful, beautiful. And all the time, *her* suffering, inside me, clawing. Till it broke.

DAVID: Are you ready then?

HELEN: We're not going yet, surely?

DAVID: It's seven now. It'll take an hour.

HELEN: I don't want to get there too early. They'll only ply us with drinks, you know how it is.

DAVID: You can always refuse.

HELEN: I don't like refusing. If people offer me things in good heart, I don't like to keep saying no. It's different for you.

DAVID: How?

HELEN: You don't mind. It quite pleases you: showing how little you need; compared with other people.

DAVID: You think I'm smug about it? I don't think so. I'm glad to feel good, I suppose I show it. There's nothing

31

wrong with that. What are you afraid of? Say it.

HELEN: I'm afraid that at some point tonight — of course it won't happen — at some point Mervyn or Anne might say: 'What value do you put on what happened, between the four of us, or between any two of us? What was its meaning, what was its significance; what has it left, what was it worth?' And I'd have to answer, if I were honest: 'Nothing. The past was not just unpleasant, more unpleasant than we knew at the time, but meaningless; without meaning. If it could all have been avoided it would have been better.'

DAVID: Not better —

HELEN: No, not even that. It would have been neither more nor less meaningful. If it had never happened.

DAVID: Then why say it? You're not obliged to be honest.

HELEN: It's true, though, isn't it? It's all the same whether it happened or not.

DAVID: It pushed us into getting some help for ourselves. Getting the therapy. That gives it point, doesn't it?

HELEN: So the only point of pain is to make us want to relieve it.

DAVID: What else?

HELEN: Nothing. Nothing.

DAVID: The present is all we have to live in. That's meaning enough, surely?

HELEN: Yes ... All the same, I hope they don't ask the question.

DAVID: They're not likely to.

MERVYN: One evening she confronted me with it. Both sitting quietly after supper, with our books — no, reading essays, I was — 'Discuss the proposition: poetry is unnecessary.' Suddenly she said, 'You're having an affair with Helen, aren't you?' I looked up; she seemed to be still engrossed in her book; our little carriage clock ticked away on the mantelpiece; a peaceful scene, domestic relaxation after the rigours of the day. 'Yes,' I said; no hesitation, no decision made; a casual answer to a casual question. She sat there still, nothing happened. I suddenly felt as if all the mess had gone out of it, all the deception, only the clean, pure, simple facts were left. There was no need to hide anything any more. Things were as they were, neither good nor bad; we had somehow cleansed the situation. A plane went over; it was the summer season, tourists were going to sunny places for their package fortnights away from it all. A cartoon came into my mind — Steinberg, I think — of an aircraft full of passengers, only he'd left the aircraft undrawn: four rows of well-dressed people sat calmly in mid-air, waiting to arrive. She was still sitting there but not reading. Her hand was across her mouth and she was staring at me. Then the questions: where, when, for how long, what did you do; what do you want to happen; very cool and calm. Cool and calm like the boffin on the beach, carefully unscrewing the detonator from the new kind of mine. Then she said: 'You know, do you, I've been having it away with David; for some time now; very good it was; is. Better than you.'

ANNE: I asked questions; he answered them; very civilised. I said: 'What do you want to happen now?' He said: 'What I *want* is to go on with it, and not hurt you. That's what I *want*.' I said: 'All right. You know, do you, I'm having a big thing with David; have been, for some time.'

MERVYN: Nothing happened then. It seemed even simpler, even straighter: she with David, Helen with me; still the foursome, still friends, no-one left out, only something added; what could be neater? What more logical?

ANNE: Which you've ruined for me, of course. For years you

had your women; now when I have my chance you ruin it for me; you realise that.

MERVYN: When it hit it hit hard and sudden. Below the belt, between the eyes; it was a knockout. I was mad, as near as makes no difference; possessed. I swore at her, pried for details, more and more details, which she supplied; was obscene, was violent. And even while she still crouched on the floor, while I still stood over her, after I'd hit her, and hit her, and hit her, I knew the justification was only in my fists. There was no logic; logic was gone. She did what I did. The value of my affair was the value of hers. The obsceneness of hers was the obsceneness of mine. The truth was the same as the lie, the beauty was the same as the ugliness. Everything was its opposite; there was no fixed point, no truth, no rightness, no logic. It was all, totally, meaningless.

ANNE: Are you going to change?

MERVYN: Do you think I need to?

ANNE: I don't know what you need. I don't know what you want.

MERVYN: What do you mean?

ANNE: I don't know whether you want to look your best or look your old self. It's up to you. I don't know why you invited them, I don't know why they're coming, I don't know how I'm supposed to behave, I don't know anything. Don't ask me whether you need to change.

MERVYN: Right. What are we eating?

ANNE: Oxtail.

MERVYN: Ah.

ANNE: I thought a bit of tail might be appropriate.

MERVYN: Devilled relationships to follow?

ANNE: Hm. So you're not changing.

MERVYN: No.

ANNE: The old self look. Are you going to be pissed when

they arrive? Or will you wait till later?

MERVYN: It's only my second.

ANNE: Your second what, quadruple?

MERVYN: There's another bottle.

ANNE: That's all right then. We can all get pissed.

MERVYN: To look my old self I'd need a face job.

ANNE: I'm surprised you didn't think of that. I wonder what we'll talk about? The kids, how they've grown up, what they're doing now; how did you find the United States? I do love the way you cook oxtail, you must give me the recipe. It's been so nice seeing you again. We did enjoy it, you must come and visit us, it'll be just like old times. Do you think we could possibly have a normal, sociable evening . . . ? I do want to see them. I really do.

MERVYN: I know you do, or you would have stopped it.

ANNE: It's just that I'm terrified.

MERVYN: What of?

ANNE: I don't know. The past.

MERVYN: This isn't the past, it's the present.

ANNE: Don't be facile.

MERVYN: There's nothing to worry about.

ANNE: Not with a bellyful of scotch.

MERVYN: Have some then.

ANNE: I think I'd better. Are you going to put that book away before they arrive?

MERVYN: What for?

ANNE: It'll look rather pointed, won't it? Reading about their treatment.

MERVYN: I told David I'd got it. I don't think they're embarrassed about it.

ANNE: Have you finished it?

MERVYN: Yes.

ANNE: Well?

MERVYN: It sounds very good. Very convincing. It makes sense.

ANNE: Do you think it works?

MERVYN: Yes, I do. I have the feeling it does. With the right people anyway. There's a lot of case histories, auto-biographical bits. You get rid of your hangups; live totally in the present. They say it's marvellous.

ANNE: Well, that's good.

MERVYN: Yes ...

> [*The phone rings.* MERVYN *takes it.*]

Hello ... Oh, yes ... tonight ... I see ... well ... yes, of course; of course you have. Thank you for letting me know ... yes, we must ... goodbye.

> [*He puts the phone down.*]

That was Simpson senior. They're switching him off tonight.

HELEN: After we got to the States I slept a lot; every spare minute. We must have seemed a rather dull couple, staying home evenings, polite but unresponsive to neighbours, watching TV, being nice to each other; I wondered whether they took us for a typical English couple. One afternoon a neighbour called in to borrow some shortening, to make a few cookies for the kiddies. I offered her a cup of tea, we sat drinking it. Suddenly she said: 'Is there anything wrong? Is there anything I can do?' Her eyes were full of concern. I wonder what she would have done if I'd told her: 'Well, you see, my husband fell in love with a great friend of mine and was having an affair with her, so I fell in love with the husband, since he was a great friend of my husband, and I was having an affair with him; but we couldn't stand that, so my friend's husband, that is my lover, left his wife, and I went off and lived with him for a while, leaving the other two to more or less live with each other as well; but this didn't work either, so I'm back with my husband and she's back with hers. Which sounds fine on the face of it, an interesting experiment in alternative living, except that on the way a few things got lost. I don't believe in love any more, for instance, or trust, or fidelity, or the sanctity of anything at all, or truth, or value, or, I'm afraid, meaning; meaning I don't believe in. I don't even believe in the innocent concern in those wide blue Country-and-Western eyes, Mrs Levington, with your nice comfy hubby who calls you honey and your kiddies and your cookies. I don't believe the world you live in is any more solid than mine. You've just been lucky so far.' But I didn't say that. I simply, suddenly, cried. And cried. And cried ... But then we found the therapy. And after a while, everything was fine.

DAVID: Time to go?

HELEN: Yes.

ANNE: That sounds like them.

MERVYN: Shall I go?

ANNE: Let's both go.

END OF ACT ONE

ACT TWO

[MERVYN, *a glass of whisky in his hand, enters to answer the phone which is ringing.*]

MERVYN: Hello ... Yes, I rang earlier, you were to ring back, was it you I spoke to ...? Yes ... I see. Well, no, I don't. Did Matron give any reason why I shouldn't be told ...? She doesn't have to know, does she ...? Yes, of course, I understand, I expressed myself badly. What I meant was, she's probably very busy and doesn't want to be bothered with ... There's no definite rule against, is there ...? I told you, I was his headmaster. And I'm a friend of his father. Well, you know, he may not feel like ringing people up afterwards ... No, no good reason. I'd just like to know when it's been done. It just happens to be — emotionally important to me ... Yes ... Yes, of course, only when you have a moment ... That's so good of you, I do appreciate it, I know how busy you must be ... Thank you so much. Goodbye ...

[MERVYN *puts the phone down, finishes his drink and pours another, as* HELEN, ANNE *and* DAVID *come in.* ANNE *has the coffee tray.*]

DAVID: It's a false problem.

ANNE: Conservation isn't important?

DAVID: I mean we state the problem wrongly. It's ourselves we have to conserve, our nervous energies. Do that and the natural resources will take care of themselves.

ANNE: I don't know what you're talking about.

DAVID: I'm saying change people, not things. It's people use the energy, not things. Don't you see?

ANNE: No, honestly.

MERVYN: Make yourselves comfortable, folks. Helen, sit there.

HELEN: Why?

MERVYN: I don't know — so I can look at you. I don't want to look at him, do I?

ANNE: Helen, would you like some more coffee?

HELEN: Thanks, Anne, I've had plenty.

ANNE: David?

DAVID: I'm fine, thanks.

ANNE: Where's your cup?

MERVYN: Buggered if I know. There, on the table.

ANNE: Was that the hospital?

MERVYN: Yes. Had to shine my charm on the little nurse. She said the Matron wouldn't like it. I said the Matron's not going to get it, dear. Bloody ridiculous.

ANNE: I don't know why you want to know, it doesn't make any difference.

MERVYN: Anyway, she's going to let me know. [*to the others*] Pupil of mine. In hospital. Well — here we all are.

ANNE: You're sure you won't have more coffee, there's plenty.

HELEN: No, thanks.

DAVID: I'm fine as I am.

HELEN: It was a lovely meal.

ANNE: It did turn out well, didn't it?

DAVID: Declicious. I do enjoy my food nowadays.

MERVYN: You always did as I remember. You've lost a bit of weight, haven't you? Don't you think so, darling?

DAVID: I eat less and enjoy it more.

HELEN: He's given up the big fat business lunches.

DAVID: Do you know, for years I stuffed myself with food every lunchtime, you know the kind of thing, taking a couple of clients to the little place I know. 'Hello Luigi, what have you got for us today?' Luigi all smarms, playing the game as hard as we did. Campari to start, brandy to finish, forgoing the sweet as if we were making a sacrifice; very jolly and important, business, you see; make friends and you make business, the firm's motto. It was a game; no business was done, we weren't such fools. One day I woke up to the fact that I hate big meals in the middle of the day, I don't *like* lunches; not under those conditions anyway. I'd been fooling myself. I stopped it. I do just as well; or if I don't it doesn't worry me. It's not a price I'd pay any more.

MERVYN: What opened your eyes?

DAVID: The treatment.

MERVYN: The therapy.

DAVID: Yes.

MERVYN: Uh-uh.

DAVID: You haven't asked me about it.

MERVYN: I shall.

HELEN: Do you remember we were always dragging you out to some new little place he'd discovered? The walking good food guide.

DAVID: Don't embarrass me.

MERVYN: We enjoyed it; you made our decisions for us, it was like having a nanny to look after us.

ANNE: Once you made me send my plate back to the kitchen. You insisted it was the wrong colour or something. 'Can't let them get away with that,' you said; I had to have something else, and I was dying for that dish.

DAVID: I must have been unbearable.

MERVYN: No, it was part of you, part of your character. It endeared you to us.

DAVID: Yet the one thing I never did was really taste the food. It was all theoretical. I didn't really *taste* it.

MERVYN: You fooled me.

DAVID: I fooled myself. There was a case of a man who always had charcoal-grilled steak. He had the therapy and

41

found he hated the taste of charcoal-grilled steak.
He'd always hated it.

MERVYN: Yes, I read about that.

ANNE: So why did he have it?

DAVID: He thought it was part of the good life. I spent my
time fooling myself, one way and another. Having
what I didn't really want, then sweating to pay for it.
That's what I was talking about, Anne. I was con-
suming energy not to enjoy the product but to placate
an inner need, a monster inside, a parasite. We sweat
ourselves silly, deplete the earth, to feed that parasite,
and it's all a waste of time; because the need is really a
need for love, childhood love; which you can never
give it, because childhood is over. What a substitute
for love, eh, charcoal-grilled steaks.

[*Pause.*]

MERVYN: Symbolic though.

[*Slight pause.*]

DAVID: Then there were the gadgets.

HELEN: Don't keep on about it, David.

DAVID: Sorry, am I boring you?

ANNE: No.

MERVYN: We'll let you know.

DAVID: You remember those gadgets I was always bringing
home? Electric potato-peelers ...

ANNE: What's wrong with electric potato-peelers?

MERVYN: That's it, David, you talk and my wife will supply the
feed-lines. What's wrong with electric potato-peelers,
apart from the difficulty of getting electric potatoes?

HELEN: David objects to *dishwashers*.

ANNE: Haven't you got one?

HELEN: Yes, but he objects to it.

DAVID: I object to the *idea* of the *necessity* of a dishwasher. [*to*
HELEN] You know what I'm talking about.

ANNE: *I* object to the idea of washing up.

DAVID: [*showing his hands*] These are dishwashers.

ANNE: [*indicating herself and* HELEN] No, David, these are dishwashers.

HELEN: He's not really a male chauvinist.

ANNE: Sounds a bit piggy to me. I bet you don't object to labour-saving devices in your office. Including your secretary.

DAVID: I do object to my secretary as a matter of fact. She's a bad secretary.

ANNE: Doesn't she do what you tell her?

DAVID: She *only* does what I tell her.

MERVYN: Lovely.

DAVID: Like a dishwasher. Like a machine. There's no joy in machines.

ANNE: There's no joy in washing up.

DAVID: There *can* be. There *should* be.

ANNE: Go and do it then. It's all out there.

DAVID: You've got a dishwasher, haven't you?

ANNE: Oh, *David* . . .

HELEN: You're being just a tiny bit inconsistent, David.

DAVID: No, I'm not. We live in the world we live in, I'll grant you that . . .

MERVYN: Very magnanimous of you.

DAVID: If a dishwasher's there and there's something you'd rather be doing you use it.

ANNE: Which is my very point —

DAVID: All I'm objecting to — not objecting, I think it's sad — is that we've come to the point where we don't like doing *anything*. We can't even clean our teeth any more, we have some electrical gadget to do it for us. We don't want to live, it bores us, we want machines to take over.

ANNE: Who's we?

DAVID: All right, I'm generalising; but it's true.

MERVYN: Vibrators.

DAVID: Exactly.

MERVYN: What a quaint old-fashioned chap you are.

DAVID: Not at all, I don't object to machinery *per se*.

ANNE: Then what are you on about?

DAVID: I'm on about something very serious actually. Perversion, the true perversion: living outside the body, which is all we really *have* to live with; living in machines; living in philosophy; living in politics; living in art . . .

      [*Pause.*]

MERVYN: How's the painting going?

ANNE: Yes, I meant to ask.

DAVID: Oh, I've stopped.

ANNE: Given it up?

DAVID: Yes. Some time ago.

ANNE: Why?

DAVID: I lost interest; just didn't want to paint any more. I never really enjoyed it.

ANNE: Then why *did* you paint?

DAVID: Oh — for something to do . . .

ANNE: Oh, come on —

DAVID: I couldn't bear not to be active, producing something. It was all part of the sickness. And for — esteem; it made me feel important. I wanted to be talented.

HELEN: You were.

DAVID: Well, maybe I was; but at what?

HELEN: You could express yourself . . .

DAVID: Express what? My hangups; my sickness; my need. I found some the other day, some drawings I'd forgotten about. Those tortured figures! The futility of it. A sick man drawing his sickness. Who for? What for?

HELEN: Then he put them in the dustbin.

ANNE: What sort of gesture was that?

DAVID: It wasn't a gesture. I didn't want them. They were of

no interest.
> [*Pause.*]

HELEN: How are you both?

MERVYN: Apropos tortured figures?

HELEN: No . . .

MERVYN: What a question to suddenly spring. All right, I'll stick my neck out: we're well, I suppose. Are we, dear heart?

ANNE: Yes, we're splendid.

MERVYN: There you are, we're splendid. Keeping our heads above water, in other words, while soldiering on through shot and shell. Cannon to right of us, cannon . . . We have, actually, haven't we?

ANNE: What?

MERVYN: The Canon living next door. Canon to right of us, going out, Canon to left of us, coming in. He's not there much, though, he goes off a lot . . . And how are you?

HELEN: I'm very well, thank you.

MERVYN: Don't thank me . . . No, you look well. As for you, David, my old mate, you're like a cat in front of the fire, a picture of self-satisfaction.

DAVID: Do you mean smug?

MERVYN: I didn't say that.

DAVID: I feel fine actually. Really fine.

MERVYN: That's good.

ANNE: It is good to see you both. I was nervous, you know. I mean at the thought of seeing you again . . . after so long . . . I mean people change, you know? Silly really . . . I mean, to worry . . .

MERVYN: I mean . . .

ANNE: Would you like some brandy!

HELEN: No, I'm all right as I am, thanks.

ANNE: For you, David?

DAVID: I'm fine.

ANNE: I know you're fine, but do you want some brandy?

DAVID: I won't, thanks.

ANNE: Darling?

MERVYN: I'll stick to whisky. Some for you?

ANNE: I might as well.

MERVYN: Darling, don't say you might as well, not with whisky, not at four quid a bottle. All the time she says she might as well. She goes through life like a depressed housewife in a supermarket: hand poised over the shelves, hypnotised by an infinity of choices, between almost identical products, all mediocre. Which shall it be? Gravity takes over, the hand falls, on a packet of Vesta curry. Might as well. She said it in bed the other day.

ANNE: And who are you, Jean-Paul Sartre or somebody?

MERVYN: Why don't you say 'Yes' to life? Or 'No' to life. You can't say I might as well to life. Well, not to whisky. If you might as well have a whisky you might as well not have it and save a bit of money.

ANNE: Mr Positive! Just give me some bloody whisky.

MERVYN: Are you mad with desire for it, is your tongue hanging out? Is it like the first time?

ANNE: Mervyn, you're getting boring.

MERVYN: Right.

[*He pours the whisky.*]

ANNE: As for the mediocrity of the product, that's *not* of my choosing.

MERVYN: What's that you say?

ANNE: Nothing. And do you really need any more?

MERVYN: If I don't need it I want it. And if I don't want it I need it. Anne's afraid I'm turning into an alcoholic.

ANNE: Don't be ridiculous.

MERVYN: You mean you're not? I've been relying on you to do the worrying for me. I have to do everything myself. This calls for a drink.

HELEN: I was a secret drinker. In the States. The country's full of them.

MERVYN: [*laughing*] I was a Secret Drinker! What was your tipple?

HELEN: Gin. I started fortifying myself in the afternoon, and then I found I was taking the bottle to bed with me.

ANNE: In the afternoon?

HELEN: We had a TV at the foot of the bed. I'd lie there through the afternoon watching the soap-opera, all those empty confrontations. I used to imagine the TV set was a kind of vivarium, full of unhappy people, crawling over one another, forced to go on and on, in spite of themselves, for ever. Then I'd start to cry with the gin, and it was as if I were in there too, crawling over bodies in that glass tank; and then, if I was lucky, it was all suddenly terribly funny, the meaninglessness of it. Oh, the relief of that. Then I'd sleep. David used to come home hoping for sympathy and a hot supper, and find me in bed, blotto.

DAVID: One day I went downstairs. I had a small hand-gun. I brought it up, and stood there for — I don't know how long . . .

[*Pause.*]

MERVYN: Well, enough chit-chat. Let's get down to the nitty-gritty. David, tell me about the therapy.

DAVID: What do you want to know?

MERVYN: Everything, Father, I want to know everything . . . ! It really works, does it?

DAVID: It has for us.

MERVYN: Yes, I can believe that. You've both changed, you know.

DAVID: I know.

MERVYN: You used to be very busy people, always busying yourselves. Now there's a kind of tranquillity — no, that's wrong, a calm, a stillness at the centre there. You've

47

stopped smoking, you're not drinking. Your voices are lower, I'm convinced of it. And you had a trick with your leg, you used to continually twitch your leg muscle.

DAVID: Did I?

HELEN: That's right, I'd forgotten.

MERVYN: You've both stopped twitching, that's what it is. I was reading that people who've been through the therapy sometimes find it quite a strain having to deal with ordinary neurotics like us. Is that true? It's all right, David, I can quite believe it. People twitch all the time, even I notice it sometimes and I'm a great twitcher. We twitch cigarettes, we twitch drinks, we twitch conversation, we twitch each other and call it making love . . . Well, it's all twitching, I suppose, according to theory, the whole of adult behaviour, a twitching away from the hurt of the childhood trauma . . . And there you sit, the two of you, twitchless and apparently — I have to say it — *contented*. I read the book, by the way. Twice.

DAVID: How did you find it?

MERVYN: Very disturbing.

DAVID: Disturbing, why?

MERVYN: The implications of it. It's difficult to explain, I haven't thought it through properly, there's something . . . What are *you* staring at?

ANNE: You didn't tell me *you* found it disturbing.

MERVYN: Well I did. Anyway, tell me all about it. You don't mind, do you? Anne thought you might be embarrassed.

DAVID: Not at all.

MERVYN: You can leave out the grisly details.

DAVID: Anything you want to know.

HELEN: He likes talking about it.

MERVYN: Good. It'll be a treat for you. Was it the book put you onto it?

DAVID: Yes; one of those lucky chances. I picked it up in a bookstore. I was at my lowest, suicidal really — if I could have been that positive. You know I had a breakdown.

MERVYN: You told me.

DAVID: I started to read it in the shop. It blew my mind. I thought, that's it, that's the way out, that's for me. Perhaps I'd have taken anything; it happened to be that, thank God. When I got home I realised I'd forgotten to pay for it.

MERVYN: And then you persuaded Helen.

HELEN: I made my own decision, Mervyn.

MERVYN: Yes, of course.

DAVID: It was the simplicity of it got us; the simple logic of it. You know?

MERVYN: I know exactly what you mean.

HELEN: We managed to scrape the money together. We're still paying it off as a matter of fact.

MERVYN: With what you're saving on drinks and smokes.

DAVID: Exactly.

MERVYN: A good business proposition. You'll soon be making a profit. Where do I sign?

HELEN: It's not something to be laughed at.

MERVYN: No.

DAVID: Have you read it, Anne?

ANNE: No.

MERVYN: What? I saw you at it.

ANNE: Well, I didn't get far.

DAVID: Why not?

ANNE: At my time of life, David, it's not easy reading a book saying how simple and pleasant everything could have been.

DAVID: It still could — there's still time.

ANNE: Hm . . .

DAVID: I think everyone should read it.

MERVYN: Come, now, you don't mean 'should'.

DAVID: No, right, I don't believe in 'should'. But I do think it's terribly important.

MERVYN: Why?

DAVID: Don't you think so?

MERVYN: I'm asking why *you* think it's important that everyone should read it. After all, you've had your therapy, you're home and dry.

DAVID: I still have to live in the world. It puts on a front, you know, a mask. After the therapy you see past that. You look at a smiling face and see the muscles holding the smile in place; you see through the eyes to the anger and resentment and fear. People are hanging on for dear life, and smiling. We're in extremity, Mervyn. We really are. I can imagine a future civilisation looking back on this one, sifting through the evidence, if we leave any, and saying: 'My God, how did they survive? How could they bear to live like that?'

MERVYN: Yes, I can imagine that. And you think you've found the answer.

DAVID: Yes, I do.

MERVYN: Goodbye, unhappiness.

DAVID: Goodbye, happiness. It's just as unreal, just as much part of the illness.

ANNE: Unreal? Happiness? Haven't you been happy ever?

DAVID: I've been neurotic. I've fooled myself.

ANNE: And now you don't. Congratulations.

DAVID: Sorry, do I sound patronising?

ANNE: Yes.

DAVID: I don't mean to be.

HELEN: I think what David means —

ANNE: Let David say what he means. I have for one or two moments in my life thought, felt, I was happy, David. A few fleeting moments in the whole long stretch of it. No more than a handful of tiny diamonds — well, all right, sequins — stitched into a — utility blanket. But at least I could say to myself later: there were these; they were real — sequins. There do exist, somewhere, sequins. Now you're saying they weren't real at all, just a neurotic fantasy. Well, and if they were, what's wrong with that, if it relieves the monotony? Why shouldn't we fool ourselves?

[*Slight pause.*]

DAVID: No reason, I suppose.

ANNE: Now you're humouring me.

DAVID: All right. The false is always wrong. The truth is always right. Happiness is a feeling of transcendence, of going beyond oneself, getting outside oneself.

ANNE: And that's wrong?

DAVID: It's false. There is no outside. There's my body, and the environment which is an extension of my body. That's all we have to enjoy, because that's all there is: our bodies, in our environment, now.

MERVYN: David, you're not suggesting an orgy?

DAVID: We are what we are: this, here. That has to be enough. There's nothing else. Nothing to reach out for. I do enjoy myself. More than ever before. I can feel myself living; now; here. I don't have to be happy.

MERVYN: And if that's not enough?

DAVID: If living in your own body isn't enough, that's the neurosis.

MERVYN: Full circle.

DAVID: The search after happiness — or perfection, or ideals, or anything else that seems to come from outside the world we live in — is to real life as pornography is to real sex.

MERVYN: I like that.

DAVID: What's so difficult? Look, I am a — an organism. I live in a physical world that supports me as I help support it. I live in space and time, in this space and in the present. Not somewhere else, or in some other time, or

51

in some other world of spiritual values. I'm here, now.

MERVYN: Yes . . . Yes . . .

HELEN: I think you've covered it now, David.

ANNE: And your mind, what about that?

DAVID: What about it?

ANNE: Oh, David, for God's sake . . .

DAVID: My mind isn't something else. It's not a traveller from outer space come to take possession of my body.

ANNE: I'm not saying it is . . .

DAVID: It's part of my body; or a quality of it, or a function of it. It's part of my sensory apparatus. It makes me aware of myself, aware of my surroundings, it allows me to communicate with my environment, recognise it and touch it. That's what I need it for and that's what it is. It does its job very well.

ANNE: So it's just a bit of the machinery.

DAVID: For living with. What more do you want?

ANNE: I don't know. Nothing: I suppose I agree with you. So why do I find your attitude so depressing?

MERVYN: Because you're neurotic, darling. Join the club.

ANNE: I wasn't asking you.

MERVYN: It's no good asking him, he's too kind to say.

DAVID: If the world your body lives in isn't enough, that's a neurosis, I've already said so. It just happens to be an almost universal neurosis, so it's assumed to be normal.

HELEN: Everyone's crazy except us . . .

DAVID: The world is crazy, that's generally accepted. All I'm saying is there's a way out of it.

MERVYN: The therapy.

DAVID: Yes. The therapy. I know it sounds simplistic: but there it is.

MERVYN: I agree with you.

DAVID: That it's simplistic?

MERVYN: That it's a way out.

DAVID: You do?

MERVYN: Don't look so surprised.

DAVID: So what are we arguing about?

MERVYN: I'm not arguing. I've drunk too much to argue.

ANNE: In vino, at last, veritas.

MERVYN: Yes, darling, if you can call this vino.

DAVID: Everyone wants to escape from the reality of just living. They want outside referees to tell them how they're getting on. They want value, they want meaning. That's what you're really asking for, isn't it? Meaning.

ANNE: Who, me? Yes, I suppose I am. Is that wrong?

DAVID: Misguided.

ANNE: There's no meaning.

DAVID: You want a yes or no.

ANNE: Yes, I do if you don't mind.

DAVID: Suppose the whole concept of meaning is meaningless? Suppose your question is unreal? We're sitting here talking; does it have meaning? Is there meaning in eating an ice cream? Or making love?

[*Slight pause.*]

MERVYN: Yes and no, in that order.

DAVID: Neither yes nor no. Living is the meaning. The meaning is living. Do you see? As soon as you come back into your own body, into your own experience, meaning stops having meaning. There's no separation between what we do and what it's for. There's only what we do. There isn't another world behind this one giving it values. There's one world; and this is it, and that's its value. There's only living.

MERVYN: You're a bit of an existentialist, aren't you?

DAVID: I'm *not* an existentialist. I'm not an 'ist'. I'm just living.

[*Slight pause.*]

ANNE: And then dying.

                       [*The phone rings.* MERVYN *goes to take it.*]

DAVID: And then dying. Stopping living. Why worry about that?

MERVYN: Hello ...? Who ...? Sorry, you've got the wrong number.

                      [*He puts the phone down.*]

DAVID: If you're living in the present you don't have to worry; and when you stop living you still don't have to worry.

                      [*Pause.*]

ANNE: I don't know whether that's very deep or very shallow.

MERVYN: Wrong. Neither. You've fallen into the same trap again, the yes or no trap. It's neither deep nor shallow. It's not even superficially deep or profoundly shallow. It's just a fact of his life. It's the way he lives. It's therefore true. It's no good, you can't fault it. What about you, Helen? You're staying very quiet. What are your thoughts on life, and death, and meaning, and eating ice cream, and — what was the other thing? What do you think about it all, behind those eyes I used to find so — enigmatic?

ANNE: Behave, darling.

HELEN: I don't want to talk about it.

MERVYN: Why not?

HELEN: And I don't want to talk about why I don't want to talk about it.

MERVYN: Fair enough.

                      [*Pause.*]

           Likewise morality.

                      [*Slight pause.*]

ANNE: What the hell do you mean, likewise morality? No, don't tell me. I don't think I want to talk about any of this any more. Ever. I don't think it *ever* does *anybody any* good. Did I ever tell you, David, the first really serious love affair I had was at University, with a very thin intellectual. I was physically precocious but mentally an innocent. And so, physically, I seduced him; and then, mentally, he raped me. I'd never needed to bother about meaning or any of that, I suppose I took it for granted that that side of things was somehow taken care of. Then he started working on me. Until one night, which I well remember, the night of a midsummer ball, stepping out in my New Look gown for a breath of fresh air and a smooch, my beau on my arm and poor man's Glenn Miller throbbing softly in the background, a nightingale even, somewhere, obligingly ... I looked up at the stars in that clear black sky and graduated. I saw them through his eyes, my true love's eyes: lumps of ... bits of ... machinery, in a limitless, pointless universe ... Three years later I was having kids and he was in a monastery.

[*Pause.*]

MERVYN: Now read on ... As I was saying; as it is with meaning, so it is with morality: an abstraction, a mystical spin-off from reality, part of that never-never land constructed, in its imagination, by a neurotic culture which can't bear the thought of nothing but the here and now because, being neurotic, it doesn't enjoy it; and which can't take the responsibility for its own actions because, being neurotic, it's rather vicious. How's that for a summing-up? So, David, in your new-won freedom, you never have to tell yourself you *shouldn't* do something you want to do — I suppose. Do you?

DAVID: I don't like hurting people, Mervyn. And I want to help my society ...

MERVYN: I'm not asking that, answer the question.

DAVID: Then you're right. Given what I've just said —

MERVYN: That a mentally healthy individual is of necessity moral.

DAVID: If you like. Healthy people don't want to hurt each

other. Why should they? They gain nothing.

MERVYN: All right, given that.

DAVID: Given that, I don't have to think in terms of 'should'. It becomes a matter of advisability. One makes one's own decisions. I wouldn't put my hand into the fire, for instance, if you bet me a hundred pounds, not because that would be avarice and therefore a sin, but because I'd prefer not to.

MERVYN: A hundred thousand.

DAVID: For how long?

MERVYN: Erm . . . two minutes.

DAVID: I'll make that decision when I come to it.

MERVYN: All right, what about — ? What if you were told, if you don't put your hand in the fire for — ten minutes, Helen there will be slowly . . . tortured to death; pincers, wires . . .

ANNE: Mervyn, darling!

DAVID: I imagine I'd do it. At least, I'd want to be able to.

MERVYN: Why?

DAVID: Because I'd rather have Helen than my hand.

MERVYN: That's good. What if — ?

ANNE: Mervyn, do you mind!

MERVYN: Shush, this is a serious discussion. What if there was an absolute choice between you being tortured to death, and Helen being tortured to death?

DAVID: It's hypothetical. I can't say what decision I'd make.

MERVYN: What decision would you want to make?

DAVID: Mervyn, you don't understand. It's not a matter of wanting to make a particular decision, only of making it as the need arises. I hope the need for that decision never will arise. All right?

MERVYN: Yes . . .

ANNE: Right, can we get off that now?

[*The phone rings.* MERVYN *takes it.*]

MERVYN: Hello . . . No, I'm afraid I'm still the person who

wasn't last time. Do you think you could try the opera-
tor .. ? Not at all.

[*He puts the phone down.*]

Now — David — What if — ?

ANNE: Darling, I may get rather angry if you keep on about
this.

MERVYN: It's all right, the torture session's over; that was a red
herring, I see that now. David — let's get it straight.
There is only the body: no outside references, no God,
no moral imperatives, no abstract values, these are all
neurotic fantasies. The healthy person lives in a state
of benevolent egoism, is that fair?

DAVID: Yes, given that —

MERVYN: Yes, yes, given that as a natural consequence of his
health he respects his fellows, likes to give and receive
love and doesn't want to hurt anyone. OK?

DAVID: Yes . . .

MERVYN: His morality, in other words, comes out of his own
body as a natural expression of his love and enjoy-
ment of the life which is the only thing he has. Right?

DAVID: That's very good.

MERVYN: I think so. Now: I'll try not to make it hypothetical.
Not 'What if you had to choose between dying and
Helen dying?' —

ANNE: Oh God, Mervyn!

MERVYN: — But — given a man in your happy situation who's
had this therapy, who's been cured of his neuroses;
and who has to choose between his own death and his
wife's; as it might be, on an overloaded life-raft or a —
Siberian sleigh with the wolves drawing closer —
which do you think, in your good judgment, he
would be more likely to choose?

[*Pause.*]

DAVID: You'd make a good chess player, Mervyn.

MERVYN: This isn't chess. It's a matter of life and death. Look.

[MERVYN *takes out a flick knife and opens it.*]
Confiscated yesterday; sharp as a razor.

[*He stands over* DAVID.]

Now, make your choice. You or her, David. You, or her.

[*Pause.*]

DAVID: All right. You win.

MERVYN: David, you're treating it like a game. It isn't a game. It's bloody serious, don't you see? Come on, she's asleep, you can say.

ANNE: Don't get unpleasant, darling . . .

MERVYN: Let me explain the state of play. White King there has the choice of sacrificing his Queen or being knocked off the board, in which case the game is at an end. What is he to do in one move? It's quite obvious. Why do you hesitate? You're not that bad a chess-player. The game is all there is, David; you can't get another life, but you can always get another Queen. Don't tell me you wouldn't want to live without her. After all, if she died you wouldn't then kill yourself, would you?

ANNE: Mervyn, that's enough!

[*Pause.*]

DAVID: I think he made a very fair point.

ANNE: Yes, David, but I think we've had enough about it now.

MERVYN: I haven't. Have you, David?

DAVID: I don't mind.

ANNE: I mind, do you mind? I find this conversation rather upsetting. It's quite ridiculous, but I do.

MERVYN: That's because you're neurotic.

ANNE: Oh, shut up.

MERVYN: More scotch?

ANNE: Yes.

MERVYN: There's nothing to it really. For the mentally healthy individual, cured of the pains of his childhood and thus balanced, non-belligerent and content to live life in the present, God is dead and there is no meaning.

DAVID: God was never alive and meaning is unnecessary.

MERVYN: Only watch out if you ever find yourself sharing a life-raft made for one with this nice sane guy: because he might just shove you out.

DAVID: And in a spirit of self-sacrifice you might just let him.

[*Slight pause.*]

MERVYN: Exactly.

[*Slight pause.*]

HELEN: You are a cheat, Mervyn.

MERVYN: I thought you were asleep.

HELEN: I was listening. What a destructive cheat you are. With your logic.

MERVYN: How? Tell me.

HELEN: Oh, the usual way. Like anyone with a gift for words. It's all in the abstract for you, all in the head. You bring things into existence by giving them names, then you argue the toss about them. And win, of course. You play with words. You're a great player with words. And you're so good at it, you almost convince us you're talking about something real. That's where you cheat. Words are not things, Mervyn, not actions, not feelings. They're just noises you make in your head.

MERVYN: Words are all we have, Helen.

HELEN: Not true.

MERVYN: To think with.

HELEN: Thinking isn't everything. Have you ever wondered how it is that when it comes to something as complex and problematical as bringing children into existence, women don't usually philosophise about it, they just do it? But my God, Mervyn, if you had the job . . .

MERVYN: I don't understand what you're saying.

HELEN: No, I don't suppose you do. It's too simple for you,

you can't do anything with it . . . You've been making fun of what we've done —

MERVYN: That's not true!

HELEN: You seem to think we've locked ourselves inside some sort of — tin castle, cut ourselves off, made ourselves safe. And round and round you go, because you feel you've been left out, looking for some chink, some flaw; some crack you can stick your stick of logical dynamite in. And blow it sky-high, and us with it . . . There's no castle. You imagine it. We're as vulnerable as you are. All we've done is make ourselves a little more sane, a little more comfortable, a little more able to cope. There's nothing to blow up, Mervyn.

MERVYN: Honey, I wasn't trying to get at you . . .

HELEN: Yes you were. Is that why you invited us? Did you think we'd hooked onto some new false faith that your logic could strip us of? You're wasting your time. We're not a couple of Jehovah's Witnesses. I suppose I used to believe in God, vaguely: I mean an ultimate balancing of the books, a final share-out where I'd get back what I'd lost and the others would pay for what they'd taken. I've lost that. I know I shall never get my own back. It's a painful lesson to have to learn; but I've done it. You can't take anything from us, Mervyn, because all we have is ourselves. Which we don't have to justify. We don't have to.

MERVYN: So much for the past?

HELEN: Yes.

MERVYN: It had no meaning outside itself. Whatever the waste and suffering, whatever the losses, it was in no way meant, or useful, or in a good cause, or redeemable; and whatsoever good things there were, whatever high and noble deeds, whatever pleasures, whatever loves, whatever raptures, that too is gone, and means nothing?

HELEN: What do you want it to mean?

MERVYN: I don't know. For Christ's sake, I don't know . . .

ANNE: Darling, do you know you're pissed as a newt?

MERVYN: Yes, I had noticed. But thank you for reminding me. My trainer. It's the big fight tomorrow, she's worried about the weighing-in.

ANNE: What are you talking about?

HELEN: Actually I think it's time we were going.

MERVYN: What? You can't go yet!

HELEN: We can, Mervyn.

MERVYN: I know you can. I mean I don't want you to.

DAVID: It's just the drive.

MERVYN: What's just the drive?

ANNE: Darling, if they want to go —

MERVYN: I don't give a shit if they want to go. I want them to stay and I want to be selfish. Is that all right?

ANNE: Oh dear, oh dear . . .

MERVYN: You haven't got baby-sitters, have you? And you're certainly not worried about the breath test.

DAVID: That's true.

MERVYN: It's Sunday tomorrow. You don't have to go to Church. You're a well-integrated couple, you can put up with us for a bit longer. Come on, stay another ten minutes for old times' sake for Christ's sake. My friends, my old friends, my loves . . .

[MERVYN *hugs* DAVID, *then* HELEN.]

ANNE: Blackmail. Sheer moral bloody blackmail.

MERVYN: I know, I know, I'm everything base. Sit down, sit down.

ANNE: Can I make you a cup of tea?

HELEN: Not for me, thanks.

DAVID: I'm fine, thanks.

MERVYN: D'you see, they're fine, they're always fine, these two.

ANNE: It's very interesting, Mervyn, that as soon as I tell you you're pissed you start playing it.

MERVYN: Oh, God, do I even act being pissed? I do, I do . . . Right, I shall now act being sober. You see how easily we change our protective colouring, we neurotics, well never mind that, I must concentrate and distil, ten minutes I said, yes? Because this therapy, David, or its implications, happen to be of vital importance to me, not to say an obsession, put it down to the male menopause if you like. The book was given me, lent me, by . . . No, I'm going off the track. Enough to say that something happened to the lender, I rang you up, I began to read the book, I rang you again to find you'd had the treatment, I arranged to see you tonight when, I find, something else is to happen to the lender — and I began to wonder whether somebody was trying to tell me something. Synchronicity, you know about that? C. G. Jung was with a patient who was telling of a vivid dream about a scarab: there was a tapping on the window. A scarab-like beetle was knocking to get in. So you see, Helen I didn't invite you *because of* the therapy, cause and effect is not so simple . . . Where was I? Yes, you said it blew your mind, David. Well, it blew mine too, though not at first. I was sceptical, as you can imagine, at my age one's lived through any number of final solutions. When I found the book talking about a *cure*, the psychiatrists' four-letter word — a *cure* for neurosis, for the neurosis of society, more or less guaranteed and all in a matter of months, I admit I thought you must be in a really bad way. It reminded me of the time you bought those awful cylindrical things to stop you smoking the easy way, do you remember? But I ploughed on, and then read it again, and much to my dismay it seemed to make sense.

DAVID: Why much to your dismay?

MERVYN: Because as you said, it makes everything seem so bloody simple. You say that's what attracted you to it: well, that's what put me off. We're very different, you see, you and I, I mean we always were different. I suppose it's the difference between the business man and the teacher: you have to do it, I just have to talk about it. So it didn't seem right; I know what you're going to say.

DAVID: What?

MERVYN: Looking for difficulty is part of the neurosis. Right?

DAVID: I think there's an element of that.

MERVYN: After all, if life is so simple what excuse do we have for making such a cock-up of it? So we construct our edifices to justify our incompetence — My God, the sheer volume of psychiatric shit the world carries on its shoulders, and all invented in less than a century. What a strange metaphor, shit on the shoulders.

ANNE: Bird shit?

MERVYN: Thank you, darling. The droppings of the theoretical high-flyers, the great auks of psychoanalysis.

ANNE: Great auks couldn't fly, darling. They only had rudimentary wings.

MERVYN: Exactly! They convinced us, though, didn't they? Flapping about across the intellectual tundra, rudimentary wings going like ninepence: My God, we cried, look at them go! Look at them fly! Freud, Jung, Reich, and all their brood; Laing levitating in the lotus position. Only none of it bloody works; let's face it, it self-evidently doesn't bloody *work*. Not one of them dared talk about a cure, not until this one. He *cures*. And why not? There's obviously something wrong with us all, as you say, look at the world. If there's one thing all the great auks agree on, one chorus that recurs in all that twittering, it's that we carry about with us, one and all, an almost intolerable burden of hangup. The shit on the other shoulder. There are those who say it's of the condition of man. I've never gone along with that, natural selection wouldn't allow it. Whatever it is, it ought to be possible to get rid of it; somewhere on earth by the law of averages there ought to be a sane person who can say: This is what is wrong with you, you idiots; and this is how I propose to put it right. And here it is in the book; the Messiah has arrived at last: case histories and all. And the words inscribed on the rock are these: Injuries occur in childhood, shock the child can't cope with. The pains are repressed and the result is a fuck-up. So don't humour the patient. Don't reinforce the repression. Don't play Freud's game. There is no original sin, no built-in trauma, people are really *nice*. Nastiness is removable. All you have to do is help the patient dig up those nuggets of hurt; make him feel them, make him accept the pain, feel the pain, scream the pain out. And all will be light and reason. And there are you two, light and reason if I ever saw it. No, I'm not being snide, I mean it. I remember you as you were: your arrogance, David, your terror of losing out, so endearing; and Helen, so funny, so bright, so hysterical. I'll tell you the real difference. We neurotics, we put on images, don't we, coats of many colours. We play parts to protect ourselves or entertain each other. We're the sympathetic characters, of course, we make sure of that; our excesses, our stupidities, our drunken ramblings, people love them, everyone loves a show. Whereas all you've got, as you say, is yourselves; no cover-up, no entertaining gloss, no funny nose or peacock-tail. All you can provide is reality, what a yawn, the reality of yourselves; which starts on the surface and goes all the way through, doesn't it? So that when, as now, Helen sees through the act I can't help putting on, her eyes fill with tears. That's good, no barriers there, no false fronts, just a living in the body in an environment

which happens at the moment to be not too nice . . .
And I look for something you've lost, you two, I admit
it, something I can use to write your therapy off; and I
can't, in reason, find it. More whisky, darling?

[MERVYN *pours himself some more.*]

DAVID: I don't really understand you, Mervyn. If you don't
believe it, why— ?

MERVYN: Of course I bloody believe it! For Christ's sake, don't
you understand what I'm saying? I haven't been able
to *not* believe it!

ANNE: Keep your voice down, darling.

MERVYN: What?

ANNE: You were shouting.

MERVYN: Darling, we don't have kids any more, do you
remember, we sent them off to make their own
mistakes. There's no Mrs-what-was-her-name to
bang on the wall. We're a settled middle-class rate-
paying couple approaching the evening of our lives
and if I can still find something in the world which
seems to be of importance to me, for Christ's sake
allow me to raise my voice a little.

[*Pause.*]

Oh, God, this is all going wrong . . .

[*Pause.*]

HELEN: Let's go, David.

DAVID: Yes, in a minute. The trouble is, Mervyn, I don't
exactly know what your problem is.

ANNE: I do. It's envy, isn't it?

[MERVYN *looks at* ANNE.]

It is for me. When I heard you'd had some sort of
therapy, which had worked, I felt a little pang of
resentment. It's awful, isn't it? So, I thought, they're
out of it; they've escaped. I'm left. It made me feel
rather inadequate, rather rejected.

DAVID: It's not like that . . .

ANNE: It is. You know that expression, 'Coming to terms with things?' You read an article about one of the various problems, how to cope when the kids leave home, how to cope with a broken marriage, how to cope with middle age; you skip to the end for the answer, since you know the problem already, and there it is: Come to terms with it. I don't think I've ever come to terms with anything in my life. I don't know what it means. They're all still there, the old battle-fields, silted over but still there, the old resentments, just below the surface like rusty bayonets. Nothing's finished. I suppose we'll take it to the grave with us, the unpaid scores, the regrets, the bitterness of all those defeats; with no idea what the fighting was all about. I shan't make a good death. Neither will you ... [*to* MERVYN] ... We'll go down cursing ... And when I step onto the further shore the first thing I shall do is ask for my money back. Of course we're envious. What do you expect? What did you expect? Why did you come? You must have known.

DAVID: We were asked, Anne.

ANNE: Of course, you were always good at coming when you were asked, weren't you?

MERVYN: Naughty darling ...

ANNE: Why, now? Lest old acquaintance be forgot, surely not; it's all the same whether they're forgot or not, isn't it? The past is not your bag, is it? Concreted over, your battlefields; the bad times, and the good times ...

DAVID: It wasn't easy for us, you know.

ANNE: I don't suppose it was. I'm sure it was very unpleasant for you, having to relive all that old stuff. It's easy now, though, isn't it?

DAVID: I don't think easy is the right word.

ANNE: What is the right word? [*to* MERVYN] You're good at words, darling, what's the right word?

DAVID: You don't forget things. You have to re-remember; it all comes back. It's a very painful process.
> [*Slight pause.*]
> I haven't rejected the past. I still think about it. It still affects me. Only I'm not bound to it any more, I've . . .

ANNE: Come to terms with it. Bully for you, David. Before you pass out, Mervyn, would you mind handing over the scotch?
> [MERVYN *pours her a drink, watches her, then looks at them.*]

MERVYN: Aren't we pussyfooting? Oh aren't we playing it safe though?

ANNE: Now darling . . .

MERVYN: Don't now darling me, darling. If there's something you want to say why don't you say it for Christ's sake in good plain English?
> [MERVYN *looks at the other two.*]
> We all fucked each other, don't you remember?

ANNE: Dar-*ling*.

MERVYN: All right, I'm sorry, that's putting it too crudely. After all, what's a bit of fucking between friends? We — *knew* one another is what I mean. We made ourselves naked to each other, we were vulnerable together, we gave ourselves to each other; we clung to one another, in desperation and in delight and in defeat. We gave ourselves away. And what the wife's asking, David, if I may interpret, is: do you remember that dead old thing, now that you're cured? Do you ever visit the grave? Is there a stone, or a bit of wood, marking a spot in the wilderness? And if there is, what have you inscribed on it for passing travellers to read? 'Here lie the remains of a neurotic attachment?' What about you, Helen? What have you done with it all? Was it a cremation, an oven job? Did you have any trouble pulverising the last recognisable bits? If I touched you now, there, or there, would you give a slight shiver as if there were donkeys on your grave? Would a two-minute silence help?

[*Pause.*]

ANNE: Enough, Mervyn . . .

DAVID: You completely misunderstand. It's not *like* that . . . It's not a lobotomy we've had. Nothing's been cut out.

MERVYN: Has it not? Where is it, then, all that experience? Show us your wounds. Are you loath to, like Coriolanus, or haven't you got any? We have, we'll show them to anyone, won't we, darling, we've no pride. We're a couple of old campaigners, with a lifetime of scars to prove it. We'll talk of old battles, restage them if you like, won't we, darling, my old comrade? Going over the top together, lying in the mud together, staunching each other's blood. We've seen service, and the war still goes on, the scars still form on scars. But where are you marked, you two, where?

[*Pause.*]

HELEN: David, I'd like to go now.

MERVYN: Oh, do sit down, Helen, do . . . Please, please, please . . . Because I haven't said it yet, I haven't got around to saying it yet. Give me a minute . . . The fellow who lent me the book, David, he was a strange, unlikeable lad. He was so — disconnected he didn't really believe in the physical world; he treated it like some kind of conjuring trick; as if he was waiting to see how it was done. Even his own body he carried around as if he were looking for its owner to give it back. Like a Martian in bad disguise. Though even a Martian would have accepted gravity; *he* didn't. I caught him once solemnly dropping his pen onto the desk like this; picking it up and letting it go. I asked him what he was doing, and he looked up in surprise, as if he were amazed there were beings in the world who thought they could communicate with him. 'Testing gravity,' he said. In the middle of a discussion of the sacred and profane love poems of John Donne, Simpson was testing gravity. I asked if it worked, keeping my temper. 'Usually,' he said. But he was no idiot; he was the brightest one there, including me I think. He had two obsessions, poetry and his motor-bike. He'd sit, picking his spots, while we analysed Shelley, then off he'd roar. He was a disruptive in-fluence, I hated him. I'd be talking about style and he'd break in: 'Is it better to write love poetry, read love poetry, talk about love poetry, or make love?' With his sickly smile. You arrogant sod, I thought, you try teaching Eng. Lit. to a bunch of sexually repressed louts. I didn't need him to call into question what we were all doing there. Stuck in a classroom with the sun shining outside, discussing words, discussing second-hand experiences, not even the experiences, too near the knuckle that, but the *style*. At least you market paper, what do I market? Then he took to hanging around after the others had gone, with his worried smell. You know that smell? Something in the sweat, nature's warning to potential mates: Do not use. He showed me some stuff he'd written; it wasn't up to much. I didn't know what he wanted of me. Then one day he brought me the book, said he'd like to know what I thought of it. I had a quick look, thought, Christ, I'm not getting into that, not with him. He kept asking if I'd read it, it was obviously important to him: I said no, not yet, I haven't had time. It wasn't till afterwards I read it properly. *Then* I saw what he'd wanted: to be cured of being Simpson, no less. What a carrot to dangle in front of the poor bugger. He probably did what I did: searched for a flaw in the argument, for a way to reject the feeling that it made

sense, felt right, seemed to work, that it might actually
be a true account, with all the bull-shit removed, of
what we are really about.

DAVID: Why not?

MERVYN: Why not, why not embrace the possibility of this
simple, sane future? Because, David, the bullshit, and
Simpson would have realised this, includes not only
the sort of neurotic clinging to past hurts that we've
been indulging in this evening, but a little thing
called art; that most refined expression of neurosis. If
the body is all there is, there's no room for art, no room
for mystery, no room for the poetic experience. Simpson wouldn't have known a thing about the sort of
antics we got up to, except from dirty books; but he
knew about the poetic experience. For poor old
Simpson the poetic experience was the only decent
thing he had in life; apart from his motor-bike. So he
had a problem, you see, and whether it was a practical
or theoretical one doesn't really matter. He saw the
dilemma: and he couldn't solve it. So he took a third
way out. Made a botch of it of course, and got stuck
halfway. And his lungs are still pumping and his
heart is still beating, unless that bitch of a nurse has let
me down, by courtesy of twentieth-century tech-
nology.

[*The phone rings twice. Before anyone can
get to it, it stops.*]

DAVID: You're talking rubbish, Mervyn. You know it. It's a
false problem. Do you think we've turned into a
couple of Philistines? There's still poetry, why not?
There's still music. I can still be made glad by it, or sad
by it —

MERVYN: Glad and sad! You're talking about *verse:* the enter-
tainment of the senses, the exchange of pleasing
sensations. That's not art, that's the bloody coach-

trade. I'm talking about that thing behind the words, behind the music, the quality you can't teach, can't criticise, can't pin down. That's what your therapy will cure us of, if it's true — and it may be; the intimations in it, the hints at something behind the fucking— practicality we're stuck in, the hints that catch your heart and fill you with wonder. What ode would you write on a Grecian urn, David? 'Heard melodies are sweet, but those unheard are sweeter?' Not on your life. 'Beauty is truth, truth beauty?' Rubbish. Keats was a bloody neurotic. We'd gut him of that neurotic nonsense, gut him of that sense of loss which is what art is all about, that sense of something missed, something just out of reach, something of wonder and value and delight that lives on the edge of experience. Beethoven and Bach could still churn out tunes, to make you glad and sad, though never to make your heart suddenly stop. Chekhov would write nice light comedies and Michaelangelo would be a happily married heterosexual. Why carve bodies out of chunks of rock when you can content yourself with real ones? And so for the rest of them ... So what should I have said to Simpson, if I'd let him ask his question? Get yourself straightened out, lad? Or should I have said: Look, Simpson, you're a spotty hung-up apology for a human being and I appreciate your distress: but you'll just have to put up with it, because that's the way someone wants you. Accept yourself, even if no-one else does. *Nil carborundum:* don't let the bastards grind you down, or they'll grind your balls off. Don't let them rip out your faith.

ANNE: Are you going to sit down, darling, before you fall down?

MERVYN: That's the wife ...

HELEN: So it boils down to a matter of faith.

MERVYN: What does, my love?

HELEN: Your argument. Leaving aside the rhetoric. You think we've lost something, which you still have; but you can't define it. You find your values threatened, but you don't know quite what they are, or why they're valuable, or what their purpose is. So you talk about faith.

DAVID: It puts you in questionable company. I always thought you were a rationalist.

MERVYN: So did I. There you are, I haven't a leg to stand on; my bluff's been called by your bloody therapy. Perhaps the world's finding its reason at last and I don't like it. The old neurosis will be toppled like the statue of a deposed tyrant, and there'll be dancing in the market place. Down with the old order. No more searching through the dead past looking for value; no more chasing after meaning, no more attempting the impossible, no more seeking the delight not of this world and no more disappointment that it seems always just out of reach; no more struggle, no more torment, never again need anyone die for a cause, or a friend, or give himself to a stranger, for no good reason . . . There'll come a voluntary burning of pernicious books by reasonable people, the end of the old neurosis. And the surviving nuts will stand warming their hands at it, watching the smoke rise, with irrational tears running down their cheeks, and nothing left to sustain them but a memory of a dead faith, and no way to express their feelings but an empty rhetoric . . .

[*Pause.*]

ANNE: Are you going to let them go now, darling?

HELEN: It's a sad image you have of yourself.

MERVYN: I suppose it is.

HELEN: You cling to that, don't you? The sadness of it. The

sadness of loss. Loss of love, loss of the past, loss of value, loss of meaning. You're a romantic, you're in love with loss. You hoard it like a miser, count it over. You worry about the loss of art, and what does art mean to you? A sense of loss. You invite us here, but not to see us; it's the past you're looking for. You can't switch it off, can you? If *you* were in charge of that machine, keeping that poor boy in limbo, you'd leave him there, wouldn't you? You couldn't bring yourself to decently end him; end him, mourn for him a little, and then forget him decently. You need him there, to use him. His loss is your possession. As for what I've done with what happened between us, Mervyn, I've done nothing with it. It's not there to do anything with. I remember it; I remember the intensity of it, the pain and the delight. But that's not what you want. You want the comfort back; the comfort of a love — it was a kind of love — that you knew couldn't last. Its loss was built in. You wanted that. And I remember us clinging together for comfort; even your voice, once, somewhere: Comfort me, Helen; comfort me. We did what we could for each other, took what we could from each other, it was necessary. But not any more; I don't need it, and I can't comfort you. I haven't written it off. When it happened, it meant what it meant. Now, it means nothing.

> [*Pause.* MERVYN *gets himself another drink. The phone rings. It goes on ringing, as* ANNE *waits for* MERVYN *to answer it. Instead, he starts talking over it.* ANNE *answers it.*]

MERVYN: Here's a thought: What if the quality that sets man above the rest of the animals, if that's where we want to be, is not the ability to make fire or words or weapons but the blessed gift of irrationality, the God-given capacity to be wilfully illogical, to be — *absurd*.

DAVID: Oh, Mervyn . . .

MERVYN: Don't laugh. It may be true. What's more irrational than the random mutation, and where would ∿e be without that? What if my neurosis is all I have as a human being, to keep me moving?

DAVID: You really do cheat. You can't win with logic so you say we all need to be illogical. You are a charlatan.

MERVYN: It's one way out.

DAVID: It won't do, Mervyn.

MERVYN: It'll do, for want of something better. *Nil carborundum.*
'Say not the struggle nought availeth,
The labour and the wounds are vain . . .'
> [ANNE *has put the phone down.* MERVYN *looks across at her. She says nothing. He turns back to the others.*]
If the worst comes to the worst, I can always buy myself a motor-bike. Joking, darling, joking . . .

THE END

Also available from Amber Lane Press

Whose Life is it Anyway? by Brian Clark

Can You Hear Me at the Back? by Brian Clark

Once a Catholic by Mary O'Malley

Look Out . . . Here Comes Trouble! by Mary O'Malley

Funny Peculiar by Mike Stott

Piaf by Pam Gems

Bent by Martin Sherman

Three One-Act Plays
  Post Mortem by Brian Clark
  Too Hot to Handle by Jim Hawkins
  Sunbeams by Rosemary Mason

*For information on these and forthcoming titles write
to:*
Amber Lane Press
Amber Lane Farmhouse
The Slack
ASHOVER
Derbyshire S45 0EB

WHOSE LIFE IS IT ANYWAY?

Brian Clark

Ken Harrison lies in a hospital bed, paralysed from the neck down following a car crash. He faces the prospect of being totally dependent on a life-support machine, realising that even the final option of suicide can be denied him. "If you're clever and sane enough to put up an invincible case for suicide," he says, "it demonstrates you ought not to die."

". . . a moving and absorbing drama about the struggle of a man for the right to die."

The Daily Telegraph

"Brian Clark has made a fascinating play out of this all too topical dilemma."

The Financial Times

THREE ONE-ACT PLAYS

Post Mortem   Brian Clark
Too Hot to Handle   Jim Hawkins
Sunbeams   Rosemary Mason

A collection of three modern comedies, each lasting 50-60 minutes in performance.

Post Mortem   Set in the modern office of a business tycoon. Helen Ansty, personal assistant to L.K. Halpin, arrives for work one morning unaware that her boss is dead. She takes over the running of the office for the day with remarkable results. — A strong leading female role plus 'voices on the phone' parts for 3-4 actors and one actress.

Too Hot to Handle   One day Suzanne discovers a cache of pornographic magazines in her husband's wardrobe. When he comes home from work that evening she confronts him with the evidence. — A domestic 'marriage-lines' comedy for two actresses and one actor.

Sunbeams   Set in London's bed-sit land. A social worker, Frances, meets Louise who runs a call-girl service from the flat upstairs. They begin to examine each other's role and function in society and realise that they are perhaps not so different after all. — A play for two actresses and one actor.

PIAF

Pam Gems

Pam Gems writes . . .
In the world of popular music, there are two giants and they are both women — Billie Holiday and Edith Piaf. Piaf, the street-waif, rickety, illegitimate, became the supreme mistress of the chanson, influencing and launching almost a whole generation of French singers. What was it about this small, dumpy woman in the plain black dress, looking like a concierge? How did she do it? In the first place she was, despite illness and personal tragedy, a supreme technician. But she was also a woman who never became inflated, never forgot her roots, and who never became involved with materialism. For her, singing was ecstasy. She believed above all in love, physical love. When she sang, she sang as a woman, as an adult. She sang of sexuality and, when the mood was sad, of betrayal: you believed her. She had been there. The accuracy and reality of her work is unique in a world usually characterised by the banal and the commercial. Miraculously, in a sentimental genre, Piaf found emotional truth. This was her genius.

"Quite stunning. A genuinely warm portrait of a woman who found relief from the frequent unhappiness in her life in the orgasmic joy of singing."   *The Guardian*

"Everything about the Piaf legend comes across with potent force."
Daily Mail